I0802579

Introduction by W. Terrence Gordon

Here, from *Forum* (Houston), Spring 1960, pages 19-24, is McLuhan's first extended treatment of his best-known theme. It precedes the series of media books he would write and publish over the following decade and dates from the period when his project for the National Association of Educational Broadcasters — it eventually formed the core of *Understanding Media* — was already in progress. The text is marked by a number of features that make it profitably read in conjunction with later treatments of its core theme:

1) A rare emphasis/qualifier respecting McLuhan's two basic types of order in experience and organization comes in his concession that it is "confusing at first for some to learn that the mosaic of a page of telegraph press is 'auditory' in basic structure. That, however, is only to say that any pattern in which the components co-exist without direct lineal hook-up or connection, creating a field of simultaneous relations, is auditory, *even though some of its aspects can be seen*" (my emphasis).

2) McLuhan suggests how his hypothesis about media effects may be verified: "Will it not be possible to test my diagnosis by careful checking, for example, of the impact of one medium upon another?"

3) Though McLuhan would later be taken to task for allegedly not respecting distinctions required by orthodox semiotic analysis, here he explicitly makes the scrutiny of such distinctions "a major issue: when does a mechanical code of transmission of information itself become a language? Under what conditions does a language revert to a code of transmission?"

The extensive treatment of these questions in the pages that follow culminates in a call for attention to McLuhan's primary interest since the earliest days of his teaching and research: “semiotics beneath semiotics,” in the phrase of the late Phil Meggs. It is a call to every educator in the form of a question: “What we must ask now is what totally new curricula and modes of organization are inherent in our new media?” — WTG

The Medium is the Message

Marshall McLuhan

It is not easy to convince a literary man that an interest in the psycho-dynamics of the printed form of codification of information is anything but malice toward literature. Moreover, he is likely to feel personal humiliation at finding that he is, in fact, quite unaware of some of the basic effects of the print form upon many of his most cherished ideas and attitudes. If I explain that radio and television are not really consumer media in the full sense that photography and film are, Madison Avenue gets upset. Personally I am not trying to upset such people. I am really trying to understand media and to discover their unique dynamics.

For a long time philosophy has been associated with systems, with worldviews, weltanschauungs, and general *pictures* of things. Since the Renaissance most methods and procedures have strongly tended toward stress on the visual organization and application of knowledge. Printing gave enormous stress to such visual process, to differential calculus, and to statistics.

But since the early nineteenth century, with the arrival of electrical problems and processes, mathematics and physics have moved away from visual organization and statistics toward dynamics, time organization, and what psychologists refer to as "auditory space." (Auditory space is that sphere of simultaneous relations created by the act of hearing. We hear from all directions at the same instant. This creates a unique unvisualizable space.)

To ask whether either the Renaissance achievement of statics or our modern conquest of dynamics is a *good thing* or a *bad thing* seems to mean: "What will this do to me?" The question seems to be a request for applied knowledge, but knowledge applied on one level, and for one person at a time.

The modern world of dynamics is an all-at-once world in which there cannot be single levels or one-thing-at-a-time awareness. This change is a very bad thing, indeed, for the previous technology and for all of us whose education represents a heavy investment of precious years in acquiring what may now be irrelevant modes of knowledge.

The Affluent Society by John Kenneth Galbraith opens with a discussion of the "vested interests in acquired knowledge," "the bland leaders of the bland" whose discourse and perception move evenly in the single lines and the single planes of "conventional wisdom." By taking an all-at-once view of our economic world Galbraith has so shocked the one-at-a-time people that the *American Journal of Economics* has reviewed the book on the assumption that it is a hoax. In the same way Parkinson's Law, in taking an all-at-once view of the operation of written forms in bureaucratic organization today, has appeared as a sort of Marx Brothers entertainment. It is in fact a multi-levelled analysis of a complex dynamic.

Scholarly decorum would seem to be merely the accidental result of the static procedure of taking one-thing-at-a-time. Such procedure in media analysis is as incapable of getting at the dynamics of a medium as are statistics in motivation study or social dynamics. Statistics can tell of a trend, provide a picture or a view or a perspective, but cannot *reveal* causes. In fact, it is only in our century that over-all data and all-at-once knowledge have so increased that we have moved toward the study of causes in personal and social operations. We are now concerned with causes not on a single plane or in mere sequence, but as a total field of interaction and interpenetration.

In media work it is important to understand the statics of the medium of statistics and their relation to differential calculus and the older Newtonian picture. For the problems we face are not static but dynamic, because of their nuclear origin and focus. Similarly, the means at our disposal are no longer mechanical but electronic. And the dominant impress which the young today receive (non-verbally) from our new technology is not mechanical or print-oriented but electronic and dialogue-oriented.

The world of production and management is today grappling with the changes in the patterns of command and of production resulting from the telephone and the complex synchronization in production resulting from the use of electronic tapes. The latter have ended the centuries-old regime of the assembly line. The end of the assembly line in the outer-world could well be a portent for the entire educational establishment.

Gutenberg provided the prototypical assembly line basis for all that followed. We may now be in the position, so far as literacy is concerned, of propping a superstructure without a base. During recent centuries we seem to have been as oblivious of this overall pattern of our Western culture as the humble tortoise is of the articulate design on its shell. It is hard to see how anybody could have been more subliminal than Western man since Gutenberg.

But the electronic age is becoming alert to the dangers of the subliminal whether in psychology or politics or education. The all-at-once, many-leveled awareness of the electronic age discourages continuation of the unexamined subliminal back-log of literate man.

In this time of co-existence, itself resulting from instantaneous movement of information, we are confronted by predominantly oral cultures like the Chinese and the Russian. These oral peoples take to electronic and nuclear modes of organization more readily than do we — with our centuries of linear and sequential training of perception. The nuclear physicists have to master the non-visual and non-Euclidean modes of order today. But since the telegraph, the press has presented a non-lineal mosaic, and so have radio and television.

My own work has tended more and more to center on the misunderstandings and clashes that occur between these two basic types of order in experience and organization: the visual and the auditory. The basic patterns for ear and eye found in most of the media are in their messages typically non-verbal. And it is even more confusing at first for some to learn that the mosaic of a page of telegraph press is "auditory" in basic structure. That, however, is only to say that any pattern in which the components co-exist without direct lineal hook-up or connection, creating a field of simultaneous relations, is auditory, even though some of its aspects can be seen. The items of news and advertising that exist under a dateline are interrelated only by that dateline. They have no interconnection of logic or statement. Yet they form a mosaic whose parts are interpenetrating. Such is also the kind of order that tends to exist in a city or a culture. It is a kind of orchestral, resonating unity, not a logical unity of discourse. It is not necessary to be satisfied with such a state of affairs once it is understood.

Personally, I feel none of the fervor in favor of such order, as an ideal to be sought for, that is not uncommon among anthropologists. My notion is that this kind of order is inseparable from electronic technology and that auditory order quickly wipes out or brainwashes visual kinds of order by subliminal action. As a teacher of language and literature I am aware of the values to be had from these in their printed form. But I am also aware that the artists, poets and musicians of the past century have unanimously abandoned visual structure in their work in favor of auditory all-at-onceness. It would seem that artists, of all media, respond soonest to the challenge of new pressures. I would like to suggest that they also show us ways of living with new technology without destruction of earlier achievement and form.

If there is one theme in all the arts of the past century it is that of the need for *relevance* in the patterns of human interests. To be out-of-touch with one's time, they have not ceased to urge, is to be irrelevant. To cultivate irrelevant attitudes and rhythms and order is to be not only futile but an enemy of one's fellows.

Prior to the cry for relevance was the idea of steadiness of perspective and consistency of point-of-view. This was the visual man's strategy and bias from Gutenberg and the Renaissance onwards. But since Baudelaire and Cézanne such individual perspective has been held to be as irrelevant as "self-expression."

It needs no insistence to show that "relevance" is an all-at-once, inclusive and total affair, and that as an attitude it is born of the *ear* mode of awareness — whereas individual point-of-view is the *eye* mode and is born of a technology in which mechanical and animal forms are dissociated. (The wheel, for example, is referred to as the classic instance of the separation of mechanical and animal form; today, with rocket and air-cushioned saucers and electronic circuits in which there are no moving parts, there is a transmutation of mechanical into animal again, as it were. We move toward the post-mechanical.)

The *ear* mode of all-at-once or *total-field* awareness seems naturally to prepare the climate of opinion to welcome organic and ecological approaches to problems of education and society, of the arts and industrial production alike.

If my diagnosis is correct, does it not afford a means of isolating causal factors and relations in our open society of over-all coexistence? Will it not be possible to test my diagnosis by careful checking, for example, of the impact of one medium upon another? Just as electronic nuclei can only be reached or probed by other accelerated electrons, cannot we use the action of the media themselves upon one another to reveal their powers and properties?

When radio is released in a widely and long-literate area like the United States its effect on social and psychological structures would seem to be quite different from the effects of radio in Japan, or Germany or Spain. But the effect of radio on non-literate areas like India, Iran or Africa would seem to be quite different again.

This approach is structuralist but is not derived from the recent field of structural linguistics. Rather it derives from the practice and criticism in the field of poetry and painting during the last 100 years. The electronic tapes which are ending the assembly line in industry also made possible structural linguistics. And this new field, as it clashes with older language study and teaching, affords another instance of the clash of ear and eye structures of knowledge. For the structural linguist the fact that the letter "k," for example, as *written*, may suggest a single sound, does not hide the fact that there are several quite distinct "k" sound-structures mastered by every child by two or three years of age. The "k" in "quick" is not the "k" in "chalk." Using the all-at-once approach of electronic tape, the linguist becomes aware of the interpenetration of the alphabetic sounds and the consequent modification of letters that look alike in the one-thing-at-a-time world of the written word. He does not hesitate to say that written letters, insofar as they pretend to point to distinct sounds, are a very crude gimmick for reducing complex and subtle qualities of sound to mere averages.

But the ear order of the structural linguist finds a clash when he turns to the visual order of words on the page. What has long passed as "grammar" to the visual and literary person seems crude and arbitrary to the ear perception of the structural linguist. Here he *could* be mistaken.

The eye-order of the printed page and of the written word, as sponsored by the grammarian, may lack the organic unity and delicacy of the spoken idiom. Eye-order may here have a validity imperceptible to the structural linguist with his subliminally-espoused ear-order via electronic tape.

But the pros and cons can more easily be tested when the real nature of the clash is clarified.

The eye man in this order of observation is satisfied that film and television images are roughly alike. Yet just as small children can make the most delicate distinction of subtle sound structures, so do they receive and react to the distinction between movie and television imagery — that is, between the still shot and the continuous pick-up, between light *on* and light *through* an image.

This illustration may serve to introduce a theme that could be crucial to understanding media. Professor Johnson of McGill University's Department of Psychology has been working on what can be called a "saturation theory" of learning. If a child can learn a language at three or four in the sense of being at home with its sounds, gestures and syntax, how long does it take a child to be at home in the same way with the structure of print, photo, film, television, radio and gramophone?

This question includes another: can familiarity or saturation with one medium block introduction to others? The child who learns one language before another will have only one mother-tongue. He will not learn the second in the same total way as the first. Carl Orff, the Viennese composer, has a music school in which he seeks to train his pupils *before* they can read or write. His view is that after literacy nobody can really master the modes of music.

This approach, quite apart from the validity of the particular case, suggests that in understanding media we might check whether the current familiarity of children with photo and television, for example, *before* they read and write may really be an unfortunate sequence. I am sure that if a more natural and fruitful sequence of media experience exists, it can be discovered and demonstrated. This approach is related to the now accepted idea that some media are especially indicated for some kinds of learning. But Johnson's theory that saturation in language and media experience occurs very early may prove of major aid in study. It certainly points to a variety of procedures and controls in observations that have been lacking.

Speaking casually to a member of the Institute of Child Psychology in Washington, D. C., I happened to inquire, "What is the effect of the telephone on children?" The reply was this: "We know one thing; namely, that neurotic children are normal when using the telephone." That remark suggests, to me at least, a basic aspect of all media: that experience in one is transmuted and translated into a different experience in another. Some people stutter in English but not in French or Spanish.

Would it not interest Bell Telephone to use their research laboratories to consider some aspects of their medium in relation to other media and to the training and education of children? That is, can we not enlist the resources of all the communication industries to concentrate on discovering the interrelation of media in terms of experience and education?

Can we not reasonably expect to interest Remington Rand and Underwood in investigating the effect of composing on the typewriter? What is the effect of publishing oneself, as it were, while composing at the typewriter? What has been the effect of the typewriter in structuring decision-making in our world? How has the typewriter been affected by tape recorders? What has been the effect of the typewriter on the writing and publishing of books and newspapers? On the short story? On poetry? On reading habits?

Much of the data about the effect of one medium on another is to be found only in the experience of the big industries. I spent a week at a radio conference in Vancouver in the spring of 1958. The theme was: What has happened in radio since television? The answers were most helpful. Radio has changed in its uses and programming since television. It has switched from a group to a private form, etc.

What happened to the book after the newspaper? To the book after the movie? To the book after radio and television? Nobody seems to know. What has happened to the movie since television is much better known, and if studied not as a change in our view of the movies but as a change in the uses and forms of the movie, much can be learned about the movie, and about television and movie at the same time; i.e., much that could not be learned by inspecting merely one-at-a-time.

The "content" approach to media and to the testing of media efficacy in teaching and in public relations and politics is, I am reasonably satisfied, derivative from the habit of literacy itself. We would not talk about the "content" of a tune or a melody. But as soon as man learned how to encode the audible in visible terms (writing) he easily began to make divisions between "form" and "content," and between thought and feeling, individual and state, and so on. Insofar as these separations correspond to real modes of being we should try to retain them. Insofar as they are fictions and illusions fostered by the subliminal action of media, they need to be considered and criticized with a view to their permanent value. Perhaps we shall learn to cherish some of the fruits of literacy as we might precious artifacts of vanished societies. Whether it be possible to retain the fruits of literacy without the soil and tree of literacy would appear to be the test we are now undergoing in the Western world. Certainly we shall learn many new aspects of literacy as we study its impact on the ancient cultures of India and China. For literacy in the West did not slice into ancient civilizations, but struck into tribal societies which wilted under its impact.

This raises a major issue: when does a mechanical code of transmission of information itself become a language? Under what conditions does a language revert to a code of transmission? With our new coding devices today, movies and television, tapes, discs, radio, teletype, and so on, we are setting about to establish whether these means of transmission have themselves so deeply altered human sensibilities and re-shaped human institutions and attitudes as to have acquired the status of new languages. For to an infant, English is not a language but a mechanical code. To an adult beginning Russian, it, too, is at first a mechanical code. It becomes a language only when it has become subliminal to him. English in its totality becomes a code again to the structural linguist who begins to translate the whole structure into auditory terms alone. To the same man as a speaker of English, it exists in all his senses at the same time.

Is a code the translation of *one* sense into another single sense; e.g., Morse code? Morse reduces the multileveled structure of English into *one* sense—the ear. It is at once translated into a code for the eye.

When writing was invented it was a visual code for a many-leveled auditory thing. Phonetic writing has proved much the most powerful of written instruments for it abstracted "all" meaning from the visual code. Other kinds of writing did not attempt to divorce the code from meaning. Once this divorce had been effected, it was possible to translate any sound structure into phonetic alphabetic form. The phonetic alphabet gave to the Graeco-Roman world the power of conquest of all cultures it contacted. We see that aggressive power today at work in India and China.

Today, by means of "translating machines" we are setting out to do with entire languages what was once done in divorcing meaning from visual written forms. When by frequency counts we have averaged out the lexical meanings of all words in a language we can use that language as a mechanical code such as it is for a beginner. When the same has been done for other languages they can be translated into one another lexically and semantically, just as they formerly were reduced from auditory to visual state by means of the phonetic alphabet.

What I am saying is that new media may at first appear as mere codes of transmission for older achievement and established patterns of thought. But nobody could make the mistake of supposing that phonetic writing merely made it possible for the Greeks to set down in visual order what they had thought and known before writing. In the same way printing made literature possible. It did not merely encode literature.

That is what I mean when I say that (in the not-so-long run) the medium is the message. What we must ask now is what totally new curricula and modes of organization are inherent in our new media?

Let us step aside from teaching for a moment and notice what the telephone and other electronic means have done to well-established patterns of management and decision-making:

> We still express the structure of authority, responsibility, function and rank in organization in the typical organization chart, which shows the chief executive at the top and the lesser executives as exercising authority delegated by him. It is still customary to explain the existence of organization by the fact that there is more work to be done than any man can do, so that he has to delegate to others what is really part of his job.

> But this is nonsense in modern organization. The individual people of skill, knowledge and judgment cannot exercise somebody else's authority or somebody else's knowledge. They exercise their own knowledge and should have the authority that befits their contribution. It is the job that determines the authority and responsibility of the holder — and this is original authority grounded in the needs and objective requirements for performance rather than in the power of the man above. The only power the top man must have is that of deciding whether a certain contribution is needed — and even that, increasingly, must be an objective decision according to objective needs of the organization rather than a power decision.

That is Peter Drucker writing in *Landmarks of Tomorrow*. Delegated authority cannot in the long run be transmitted or used by telephone. The decentralization of industry that has followed upon the breakdown of delegated authority has compelled industry to give to all its executives an over-all training in the entire operation of their companies and also compelled the study of the entire relation of business to society. In Nazi Germany the clash between delegated authority and electronic transmission was given a brief moment of attention by Albert Speer at the Nuremberg trials:

> The telephone, the teleprinter and the wireless made it possible for orders from the highest levels to be given direct to the lowest levels, where, on account of the absolute authority behind them, they were carried out uncritically; or brought it about that numerous offices and command centers were directly connected with the supreme leadership from which they received their sinister orders without any intermediary; or resulted in a widespread surveillance of the citizen; or in a high degree of secrecy surrounding criminal happenings. To the outside observer this governmental apparatus may have resembled the apparently chaotic confusion of lines at a telephone exchange, but like the latter

> it could be controlled and operated from one central source. Former dictatorships needed collaborators of high quality even in the lower levels of leadership, men who could think and act independently. In the era of modern technique an authoritarian system can do without this. The means of communication alone permit it to mechanize the work of subordinate leadership. As a consequence a new type develops: the uncritical recipient of orders. (Albert Speer, German Armaments Minister in 1942, in a speech at the Nuremberg trials, quoted in Hjalmar Schacht, *Account Settled*, London, 1949.)

Speer does not dissociate the effect of electronic media from some of the special features of German cultural organization. And, for example, what he notes about the older type of organization—that it calls for "men who could think and act independently" — is quite the reverse of the situation seen in United States business by Peter Drucker. For the new situation in America is precisely the one that calls for such "authority of knowledge," whereas the older literacy, at least in the United States, fostered the pattern of delegated authority. What seems to have occurred in Germany and Japan under electronic impact was the brainwashing of a recently assumed literacy and reversion to tribal cohesion and pre-individualist patterns of thought.

I have said (and I hope I am wrong) at various times that we ought to expect a steady trend toward irrational tribal behaviour in North America, as our youngsters get saturated with the all-at-once auditory experience of our new media. Such tribal experience was still intact and available to the Japanese and the German. But for us to retribalize would be quite a different matter. And in the global village created by our electronics there would, of course, be room for only one tribe — the human family itself.

It would seem obvious that our responsibility as educators or as broadcasters is to understand our media and their effects just as an expert should understand the effects of his medium and not permit patients to receive an overdose. X-ray units can get "hot" but they do not make good space-heaters. And we must learn how far we can safely proceed in applying new media to older educational purposes without destruction of older goals and achievements.

Moreover, since the saturation in a medium may occur outside school contexts before any school use is attempted, we must know what are the relevant educational uses of such media. "Saturation" in English as the mother-tongue occurs by three or four years of age and the traditional educational superstructure is based upon that prior saturation. Have we used a similar wisdom in relation to the new media? As they cease to be codes, and invade and structure all areas of our sensibility, they become "languages" themselves.

Pictorial media tend to be non-verbal, it is true. But so are writing and printing non-verbal in their primary phases. Only gradually do they permeate the verbal and spoken areas. The Morse code if known and experienced daily by everybody would quickly cease to be a code. The African drum and whistle languages are not codes but languages to African natives. So with their dances. Ads, comics, and movies are not codes in North America but basic languages. That we have not yet begun to teach their grammars is as natural as it is for pre-literate man to ignore the written or visual mode of his language. Grammar comes from the Greek "written." And education would seem to involve the translation of experience into a new mode.

We can begin, then to consider the relevance of grammars for media which have become languages all within our own century. Whatever may be the educational advantages of traditional grammars now apply to our new media. Yet one of the effects of the new auditory media has been to dissuade people from the cultivation of grammar. May it not be that the translation of the auditory structure of a language into a grammar or visual structure is ultimately necessary in order to confer personal adequacy of control over experience? But as we regain auditory space via the electronic revolution, we fail to see the relevance of visual grammar?

May not the translation of one sense into another, and of one language into another, be the irreducible modality of education, just as it is the irreducible mode of nuclear investigation? May not this training confer the detachment and criticism necessary for viable civilized man anywhere, anytime?

For the Greeks numbers were indications of auditory structure, not visual structure. Ernst Cassirer in *The Problem of Knowledge* tells us how the vogue of Euclidean geometry depressed and retarded the study of numbers and arithmetic for centuries. Today the effect of new auditory modes on the young will naturally sensitize them to number theory in a way which is taken for granted in old oral cultures like Russia, Hungary, Poland, etc.

Today it is impossible to predict at what moment one may make a large break-through into new dimensions of awareness. Such a casual fact as that the sound waves on the wings of a jet plane become visible just a moment before breaking through the sound barrier may be encountered for the first time in a newspaper or in overheard chat. It has profound implications for the dynamics of sight and sound and tells us much about their power and habit of transmutations. The radio tube principle, pushed far enough, led to television.

It was Flaubert in the middle of the last century who first alerted his time to the subliminal power of bad pictorial forms. His people are all shown as victims of atrocious commercial art and communication. His own concept of *le mot juste* (which our age translates as *The Most Juice*) is auditory, not pictorial. For it implies an all-at-once order of words, any slight change in which obliterates the whole effect. But Flaubert taught us that there is no neutral area in human communications, and no more merit in tolerating hideous and tendentious forms of pictorial arrangement than in putting up with polluted drinking water. Before Pasteur, Flaubert introduced the germ theory into social communication. That is, he entered the electronic age at the same time as Sam Morse. But Flaubert had his eyes open for the full consequences as Sam Morse, perhaps, did not. It was probably no accident that Morse, a painter, should have been the first to introduce us to auditory or all-at-once space, the space which is a simultaneous field of relations such as we create in each moment of hearing. For we hear from all directions at once; we do not see that way at all.

—Marshall McLuhan, one of the editors of the distinguished Canadian journal Explorations and the author of The Mechanical Bride, teaches at St, Michael's College at the University of Toronto.

The Medium is the Message
Marshall McLuhan - Unbound (17)

ISBN: 1-58423-051-7
Library of Congress Control Number 2005927213

Marshall McLuhan Unbound Project Editors
Eric McLuhan, W. Terrence Gordon

Published in United States in October 2005 by
Gingko Press, Inc.
5768 Paradise Drive, Suite J • Corte Madera, CA 94925
(415) 924-9615 • Fax (415) 924-9608
email: books@gingkopress.com
http://www.gingkopress.com

Design, packaging and production: Die Gestalten Verlag, Berlin
Layout and Typography: onlab, Berlin
Fonts: *Dolly* by Underware, *Bullet* by House Industries
Production: Martin Bretschneider, Vinzenz Geppert
Art direction: Robert Klanten

Made in Germany